T0050674

The Little Manual of
ENLIGHTENMENT

First published by O Books, 2009
O Books is an imprint of John Hunt Publishing Ltd., The Bothy, Deershot Lodge, Park Lane, Ropley
Hants, SO24 0BE, UK
office1@o-books.net
www.o-books.net

Distribution in:	
	South Africa
	Alternative Books
UK and Europe	altbook@peterhyde.co.za
Orca Book Services	Tel: 021 555 4027 Fax: 021 447 1430
orders@orcabookservices.co.uk	
Tel: 01202 665432 Fax: 01202 666219	Text copyright Vikas Malkani 2008
Int. code (44)	
	Design: Stuart Davies
USA and Canada	
NBN	ISBN: 978 1 84694 163 4
custserv@nbnbooks.com	
Tel: 1 800 462 6420 Fax: 1 800 338 4550	All rights reserved. Except for brief quotations
	in critical articles or reviews, no part of this
Australia and New Zealand	book may be reproduced in any manner withou
Brumby Books	prior written permission from the publishers.
sales@brumbybooks.com.au	
Tel: 61 3 9761 5535 Fax: 61 3 9761 7095	The rights of Vikas Malkani as author have bee
	asserted in accordance with the Copyright, De
Far East (offices in Singapore, Thailand,	signs and Patents Act 1988.
Hong Kong, Taiwan)	
Pansing Distribution Pte Ltd	
kemal@pansing.com	A CIP catalogue record for this book is availabl
Tel: 65 6319 9939 Fax: 65 6462 5761	from the British Library.

O Books operates a distinctive and ethical publishing philosophy in all areas of its business, from its global network of authors to production and worldwide distribution.

This book is produced on FSC certified stock, within ISO14001 standards. The printer plants sufficient trees each year through the Woodland Trust to absorb the level of emitted carbon in its production.

The Little Manual of

ENLIGHTENMENT

7 Valuable Tips for Those in Search of Awareness

Vikas Malkani

Best-selling author of

THE LITTLE MANUAL OF MEDITATION

BOOKS

Winchester, UK
Washington, USA

There are many paths to enlightenment.
Be sure to take one with a heart.

Lao Tzu

This book is dedicated to all the
great Masters who taught me in spirit:
Krishna,
Buddha,
Jesus Christ,
Lao Tzu,
Paramahansa Yogananda,
Ramakrishna Paramahansa,
Ramana Maharshi,
Osho,
Swami Vivekananda,
Eknath Easwaran,
Ramesh Balsekar,
Wayne Dyer and
Deepak Chopra.

And most of all to the Masters who taught me
both in spirit and in form:
Swami Rama of the Himalayas,
Sadhu Mukundjivan Dass of Yogi Divine Society, Delhi, India,
Pappaji of Gunatit Jyot, Gujarat, India and
Swami Hariprasadji of Haridham, Sokhda, Gujarat, India.

I bow in humility before you all!

The experience of enlightenment transformed
my entire life and purpose of being.
From that day on, it became my endeavour
to guide as many people as I could
to their own truth and completion.

I am indebted to you dear reader
that you have given me a chance
to do so with you by picking up this book.

Testimonials for Vikas Malkani
and His Teachings

Vikas is able to capture in words what can only truly be felt by the heart. A state of being, without limits, is captured beautifully in this book…and for this I am eternally grateful.

Sally Forrest, International Reiki Master and Teacher

I try to meditate twice daily and I have been doing it for about two years now. I feel calmer, more joyful, more grateful for everything, I sleep better. I am able to 'see' that, with LOVE, all fear dissolves.

On the physical level, I am sleeping better, I feel better. I feel more aware of my body's needs and I have better discipline. On a much more subtle level, I have become aware that I am not my body. I have become more aware of my emotions and my thoughts as they arise. While I am generally calmer, quieter and more centred, I have also become more aware of my surroundings, the people around me, their feelings and their motivations. I find myself more giving, more loving, more accepting.

A lot of issues get resolved without apparent effort. I am more able to 'let go'. I don't get so upset and agitated when I don't get my way or when I feel confused. Meditation somehow brings about the dissolution of the problems automatically. I am much more aware that God is with me all the time. I don't have to worry, I can relax.

Sanne, housewife, mother, spiritualist, Singapore

am connecting with myself through meditation, becoming whole
nd complete. Meditation has led me to develop awareness,
etachment and a joy of life. I feel connected to a higher force. I
m joyful and at peace. Meditation is an essential life skill and
ikas is an outstanding teacher.

Deepa Chatrath, India

hanks so much for an enjoyable and en-light-ening teaching
lled with e-motion and insight. Vikas' teachings are heart-centred
nd go beyond the mind, helping us to be the master of our minds.
is so simple, logical and has been proven by the ancients. Vikas
rries a message of truth because it comes straight from the heart.

Lynn Ogden, Hong Kong

ikas' teachings brought all the pieces of the jigsaw puzzle
)gether. It has provided me with a solid basic foundation on
hich I can build my spiritual journey. The teachings were lucid
nd practical. I thank Vikas for his guidance and look forward to
:arning from him in the future as well.

Anne Chapman, Hong Kong

he teachings given by Vikas are most inspiring; they lead me
) think deeper. His teachings are simple, direct and easy to
nderstand. I look forward to learning more from him.

Pauline Wong, Hong Kong

Contents

Author's Note

Enlightenment is your birthright! Let me show you ho to arrive there.

Each one of us is on a personal journey. This is a journey tha is significant and truly memorable. For, the journey is a important as the destination. Actually, if you really look dee enough, you will soon realise that the journey and th destination are the same.

As I have said above, enlightenment is our birthright. All of u are headed towards this delightful state; some of us are er lightened without even realising it. Sometimes it takes man lifetimes to reach this state; often, it appears to have happene in one glorious moment.

Yet the word 'enlightenment' continues to baffle us. We look a the great spiritual leaders and declare that they are enlightene souls. But we fail to look within and declare that we, too, are i constant touch with our Creator; that we, too, may well have de veloped spiritual insights that help us see the light. Here, w need the guidance of a teacher and the grace of God.

This manual is not a complex book on a complex and difficu

grasp topic. On the contrary, here is your complete guide to
nlightenment or, should I say, here is the state of enlightenment demystified. These seven valuable tips will make you more
spiritually aware and lead you to a stage where you can easily
connect with the higher power.

ikas Malkani

Chapter One

Do Not be in a Hurry

Enlightenment must come little by little, otherwise it would overwhelm.

Idries Shah

Without strong roots, a tree cannot bear good fruit. Or imagine a very tall building, which is built by adding one floor upon another; it is only as strong as the foundation that holds it.

If your grounding in the basics of spiritual awareness and knowledge is not strong, then everything else that you add on to it as you progress in your own evolution has a chance of crumbling with pressure or confusion.

Most of us live out a conditioned behaviour about life itself— we run it as a blind race that we see everyone around us running. It is this same tendency that we adhere to when we enter the realm of spirituality; we take it to be a race.

In any race of the external world, whether it is a race for money or fame or power or even a race for relationships, we attempt to finish something or acquire the maximum in the shortest and fastest way possible. Since we are so conditioned and comfortable with running races in the outside world, we carry the same tendency with us when we enter the world of our inner life. We nter into the realm of spiritual wisdom and all we want to do is hurry to the end.

n total contrast to this, my Master would remind me repeatedly, "Do not be in a hurry, especially in the beginning." Make sure that your foundation, your root, your beginning, is very, very strong. When that is strong, then everything that is added on to that is already standing on a firm footing.

> ✫ Once the foundation is laid and stands strong in its own being, it can support great height upon itself ✫

Once the foundation is laid and stands strong in its own being, it can support great height upon itself.

At this point, some of you may say that you pray and meditate regularly, you have read all the scriptures, you accept that divinity is literally everywhere and in everything, then why does it take so long for our realisation or experience of it?

This is the first requisite of a seeker—never, ever, be in a rush. Keep in mind that enlightenment happens often when you least expect it. But it will happen, you will arrive at this state of nirvana, take my word for it.

As an initial step, you should, at all times, be open to receive the light of God's wisdom. You should be full of longing for it; you must yearn to connect with your Creator.

Sri Ramakrishna, the enlightened Indian Master, had narrate
the story of a disciple who asked his teacher to help him se
God. To this, the guru replied that if the disciple came with him
he would certainly show him God. He took the disciple to a lak
and both of them entered the water. Suddenly, the teache
pressed the disciple's head under water. He released him afte
a few moments and asked him how he felt. The disciple replied
"Oh! I thought I would die; I was panting for breath. I coul
think of nothing else."

The wise teacher then said, "When you feel like that for Goc
then you will know that you haven't long to wait for His vision

Be desperate for the light that comes with God and you wi
surely see it. Crave for it as you would for none other. Realis
that divinity is everywhere; there is no place where God is nc
present. This is the truth and all the scriptures of the world stat
it.

The Upanishads are ancient manuals on the spiritual journe
and the nature of divinity that were written thousands of year
ago by enlightened teachers. I am certain that many of you wh
have read these scriptures are familiar with the concept men
tioned in the Upanishads: "There was only One and the On
became the many."

The Bible says, "The kingdom of heaven is within you." I
the ancient scriptures of India it is written, "God is within an

ithout." And the beautiful Upan-
shads reiterate, "There is only One
nd the One is everywhere and in
verything!"

f this were the truth, then this would
nean that God is within you but,
t the same time, outside of you,
verywhere around you and in everything, too. You can find
he Creator in the person that you see before you in this
noment, in the entire nature around you and in every small
art of the universe.

> ☆ Be desperate for the light that comes with God and you will surely see it. Crave for it as you would for none other. ☆

Different religions state the same truth in different ways. The
Bible, supporting this belief, states, "First there was the word.
And the word was with God. And the word was God."

n the Upanishads it is stated as an experienced truth that
ssentially there was only One before everything else and that
One became the many. And once the One has multiplied into
he many, what do the many do? Well, the many merge back
o the One. The seers say that this is, in fact, the process of
he beginning and the end of the whole cycle of creation.

But, the real question for someone on the path to the truth is
his: If there was only One, and the One became two and the
wo became many, what is stopping us from going back? Why
an't we reach our source?

What keeps us away from God or our true self? Why is it no possible to have this realisation of the eternal divinity rig now? What prevents this union between man and God? Wl cannot the omnipotent, omnipresent and omniscient Creato and the source of all things, even of me, reveal itself to me i this very moment?

There are many people before us who have had this realisatio who have experienced the divine. Then why not us? Why n *now*? Why do we need to wait?

Why is it not possible in this very instant?

Or is it?

This is a very relevant question and something that we need answer for ourselves. But before we can move on we must kno one thing very clearly: What are we after?

We are after the final realisation of our true self, our mergir into the divine.

We want to know what God is, who and what am I. We want know all that is around us. We want the final merging into t tality, the union of our small limited selves into the limitless.

We want the experience of Jesus, the nirvana of the Buddha an the Samadhi of Patanjali.

We want total and limitless unconditional love. We want the light of knowledge. We want liberty; a complete freedom from all the chains of our mind. We want to see and know that we are life eternal. We want to know our nature as true laughter; bliss and joy without measure.

Is it not possible to have this realisation right now? And if not, then we must know 'why not?'

Remember, what keeps us away from this experience in this very moment is our own concept of a separate self. As long as I keep thinking and identifying with myself as 'I', I will not be able to cross my own boundaries and see my source. I cannot meet God unless I can give up 'I' altogether.

> ☆ Let there be no boundaries between the 'what is' and 'what can be' in your mind. ☆

I cannot attain enlightenment unless I leave the 'I' behind. The gap between the probable and the possible is only as large as we make it.

American tennis coach Vic Braden had once observed, "The moment of enlightenment is when a person's dreams of possibilities become images of probabilities." Let there be no boundaries between the 'what is' and 'what can be' in your mind. Yes, you can give up yourself right here, right now. And by doing that, you arrive at your true potential.

Now is the best time to wake up to a higher knowledge. It is al
the best time to connect with the wisdom of the Creato
You have to understand that if there is only One, then there
nothing else. If there is only one Creator, which becam
the many, even then, there is nothing else. That One exists
the many.

If there is only one ocean, then all the drops of water fro
that ocean, no matter how numerous, carry the essenti
qualities of the ocean itself. In fact, every drop of water is
miniature ocean by itself.

The way I see it, we are like waves; we are a part of the ocea
an intrinsic part, no doubt, for the ocean is our source. We a
all one for we all spring from the same source.

How difficult is it to realise this? Also, how difficult is it
know this?

It is as difficult as we want it to be! We can spend an enti
lifetime understanding this truth before we accept it, or w
can simply accept it in this moment.

It is up to us.

What stops us from accepting this truth of divinity is ou
identification with our own small self. As long as the drop
water continues to hold on and identify with its identity as

rop, it can never merge itself into the ocean. In other words, can never become the ocean.

s long as we are full of our own think-ng, our own ideas, our own precon-eived notions about life, about people, ven about God, as long as we identify ith this identity of each of us being a eparate person and different from veryone else in our universe, we don't ave space within us for God to enter.

☆ Now is the best time to wake up to a higher knowledge. It is also the best time to connect with the wisdom of the Creator ☆

his space inside, the silence that exists in the recesses of our oul, is where we can hope to find our Creator. But do this seek-ng slowly, one deep breath following another equally deep one. omewhere between these deep breaths you will connect with our God and understand the wisdom of God. And the world ill change forever.

Tip 1

Take it easy

A seeker is never in a rush

Chapter Two

Stay Empty

Men go fishing all of their lives without knowing that it is not
fish they are after.

Henry David Thoreau

L et me start this chapter with a small anecdote, one of m
favourites. It carries a strong yet simple message for ou
journey to self-realisation.

There was once an English professor—a professor of religio
well versed in all the scriptures and inspirational books of h
day. He had graduated from the best religious institutions an
boasted of a photographic memory that allowed him to re
member all the verses of any scripture he had read only once
The professor was even able to expound on them with all th
knowledge he had collected in his mind over the many years o
his life.

One day, he realises that he needs extra publicity and media a
tention. His analysts and consultants advise him to meet an
debate with a very well known Zen Master. So, his secretary cal
up for an appointment with the Master and asks whether it
possible for him to debate the scriptures with the professor.

The Master, knowing very well that spirituality is not a matte
of debate, agrees. On the appointed day, the professor arrive

nd is invited into the private room of the Zen Master. The Master asks him to sit down, picks up an empty teacup, puts before the professor and asks, "Will you have a cup of tea ith me?"

The professor readily agrees.

The Master picks up the pot of tea and arts to pour the tea into the cup placed efore the professor. He keeps pouring nd pouring till the cup is full right to te brim and the tea spills over on to e saucer, and then the table, and nally on to the lap of the professor. At is incredulous behaviour of the Zen Master, the professor gets up and rushes the tea off his lap and says, What are you doing? Please stop."

The Master asks, "Why?"

The professor replies, "Are you blind? Can you not see? The up is full and everything is spilling over."

t this point, the Zen Master tells him, "Are you blind? Can you ot see? Just like this cup, your mind is also full of your own leas, of all the information you have collected in these past ears, of your own notions and your own knowledge.

☆ This essential emptiness within us, which slowly fills up with divine awareness through experience, is actually one of the secrets of coming to enlightenment ☆

Where is there space that I can put in something new?
Everything I give you will spill over."

This emptiness of the teacup is the secret of it being filled
up. The emptiness is the reason that the cup can receive and
hold the tea. Once the cup is full, once the emptiness has left
it, it can hold no more and all that is poured into it will
spill over.

This emptiness is something that we leave behind when we
enter the realm of the inner world and begin to walk the
spiritual path. In fairness, we do begin walking the path with
this emptiness as we do not find sufficient meaning or stability
in the external and material life. But as soon as we are on the
inner journey, we start accumulating so much knowledge,
so many ideas and so many teachings, that this essential
emptiness is forgotten.

The race starts all over again, only this time it is an internal
race; the race for knowing more, reading more books,
listening to more Masters, attending more workshops and
meeting more and more teachers.

This essential emptiness within us, which slowly fills up with
divine awareness through experience, is actually one of the
secrets of coming to enlightenment. Unfortunately, it is
something that we often lose when we are on the journey in a
blind way.

Instead of trying desperately to fill yourself up with the things of this world, stop for a minute, step back into yourself and create some space here. That is all you have to do. Instead of your constant fervent grasping at material and inanimate

> ☆ Prepare the ground and wait for the seed. Prepare yourself and wait for God to come into you ☆

things, relax, open your hand and just be ready to receive.

Prepare the ground and wait for the seed. Prepare yourself and wait for God to come into you. That is the best that you can do.

All the spiritual practices of this world are meant for just that —to make you ready to receive, to prepare you to hold; they are not meant to give you God. No one can do that but God. When it is God's will, your Creator shall come into you. In fact, the entire universe will conspire to make things happen just the way you want them to. But for that you must first make yourself ready, for that is the role and responsibility of a sincere seeker.

Seek and you shall find; ask and you shall receive; knock and the door shall be opened unto you—these are the words of a true Master.

This is the same truth that is emphasised in all our ancient scriptures, no matter from which part of the world they come.

You can do something, too, to help speed up this preparatio because it is our will, consciously or unconsciously, that o Creator has not come into us so far and made us enlightened souls. We have filled ourselves up so much wi what we already have that there is no space for anything n to enter. This is the simple key and God has been repeati this secret to us again and again in many different wa throughout the ages from the words of different seers. V just don't listen! We pray, we meditate, but we do not becon enlightened. And then we wonder why this is so!

Prayer is said to be the stage when you talk to your Creato meditation is when your Creator talks to you. Ar enlightenment happens when you both talk to each other. S prepare yourself for this intense, private and intern dialogue. It will happen, but only when you are ready for All of you who have been involved in relationships—lon term relationships of any kind—might be familiar with tl words heard from your partner, "You just don't listen to me Well, God says that to us all the time, too, "You just dor listen to Me."

We pray to God but, then, we forget to listen to the answer. V ask questions and then we move on, without waiting for the a swer to arrive. We simply move on to another question.

Read any scripture of any religion in this world and you sh find that divinity has always been available to you. The on

ing that is required for you to create
that little space for God to come in.
Vithout this, it just cannot happen. To
reate that space for God within you, you
ave to let go of, and surrender, your own
elf, your own small identity. Till you do
ot surrender your own self, you do not create that space.

> ☆ Emptiness is the key; it is the journey as well as the destination ☆

Remember, emptiness is the key; it is the journey as well as
he destination.

The path to divinity is not walked by filling yourself up with
nore and more knowledge and things; it is, in fact, walked by
mptying out your inner self of everything that is not needed
here for God.

our attempt should not be to fill yourself up more; your
ttempt should be to empty yourself as much as you can.

mpty yourself of your past conditioning, your ideas and
otions of God, your limits and boundaries, your old
nowledge and all the chains that keep you bound to your
gical mind.

od does not like limits because divinity is limitless and
oundary-free. Be very clear that we took to the inner journey
ecause we felt empty. All of us have experienced this empty
eeling at some time or the other. In spite of having all that

life can offer in terms of material rewards and comforts, w
find ourselves looking for something else; something mor
meaningful, more solid, more unchanging. We feel hollov
unhappy, dissatisfied and have a sense of emptiness withi
us. We want something more significant, something mor
permanent, something that does not change all the time
something that will make us stable.

The emptiness that is there within calls to be fulfilled wit
something that is true and forever.

However, as soon as we begin the inner journey, the path t
our real self, that emptiness vanishes because now we sta
picking up different concepts, ideas and knowledge to fi
that emptiness with. We forget that all of this is not God. Wha
we want is not more information, not more knowledge, no
more credentials; what we want is the direct experience an
realisation of divinity and God within us.

The man who has 'realised' is very different from the ma
who is simply knowledgeable. You can find millions o
knowledgeable persons in this world but you will fin
very few who are realised or who have experienced Go
within themselves.

Keep in mind at all times that the goal is to *experience* Goc
not to collect more knowledge or information about Goc
Enlightenment brings with it great spiritual insight

Paramahansa Yogananda shared his many experiences with his readers in *Autobiography of a Yogi*. Here is one in which, he explains, he perceived the unity of the eternal light, behind the painful dualities of delusion.

☆ The man who has 'realised' is very different from the man who is simply knowledgeable. ☆

The year was 1915 and Yogananda was meditating in a small room in the attic, reflecting on the death toll that World War I had brought. As he closed his eyes in meditation, his consciousness was suddenly transferred to the body of a captain in command of a battleship. A huge explosion took place and tore his ship asunder. He jumped into the water to save his life. But then, a stray bullet entered his chest and he thought he had died. At this moment, Yogananda found himself seated in a lotus posture in his room. Relieved that he was indeed alive, he found his consciousness transferred back to the captain's dead body. "Lord," he prayed, "am I dead or alive?"

"A dazzling play of light filled the whole horizon," writes Yogananda. "A soft rumbling vibration formed itself into words:

"What has life or death to do with Light? In the image of My Light I have made you. The relativities of life and death belong to the cosmic dream. Behold your dreamless being! Awake, my child, awake!"

Enlightenment teaches us that there is no life and no deat
The world, as we know it, just does not exist. Everything
but a cosmic drama being played out by our Creator. This is tl
wisdom that we have to seek; this is the knowledge that v
have to understand and imbibe into our subconscious.

Once we adopt the role of the aspirant, when we set out
seek, when we want to achieve God, it is very important fe
us to have great clarity of mind. This is called *vivek* in Sanskr
the ability to discriminate between the real and unreal, betwee
right and wrong, between truth and untruth, between what
required and what is not.

We need to have proper clarity of what we want and what we c
not; we need to be aware at every moment of what we have con
here to do and keep our goal in clear vision.

All of us have been provided with a limited amount of time. '
make the best use of that time does not necessarily mean to ru
the spiritual race as we have been running other worldly rac
in the past.

The spiritual goal is the highest goal of human life. To arri
at self-realisation, we will have to progress patiently wi
perseverance and keep our foundations and basics on tl
path very strong. We will have to practise the three Ds in eve
day of our life and in everything that we do: Disciplin
Devotion and Dedication. This is how we make the soil of o\

eing ready to receive the seed of divinity within us. When you ere children, do you remember how you learnt the alphabet om your teachers hundreds of times in school? They would ach it to you again and again and again—A, B, C, D, E—all ne way down to the Z. And then they would ask you to repeat again and again and again.

Vhat was the purpose of this?

was so because once you remember it, once that foundation strong, then for the rest of your life, you do not have to arn it again. It does not have to be taught to you again. stays with you forever and builds the base on which ll else can be supported. Once your alphabet is strong, nen you can learn how to string it ogether to make words, and then om words you can make sentences. nd once sentences are mastered, ou can write entire books like this ne. But it all begins with the simple lphabet. This reminds me of a aching story:

☆ Enlightenment teaches us that there is no life and no death. The world, as we know it, just does not exist. ☆

he boy sits at the Master's feet and asks, "Tell me the secret o be happy."

he Master looks at the eagerness in the eyes of his student nd responds, "The secret to finding happiness in life is not complex. In fact, it is very simple; just as simple as your ABC and Es. You don't need any fantastic secret of the hidde schools to find happiness, just follow these steps and you w find that happiness is a constant companion in your journe of life."

The Master goes on to highlight the ABCDE of happine that would help his young student to embark on the path right living and enlightenment:

Avoid negative people, places, habits and sources.

Believe in yourself and your dreams.

Choose to work for what you deserve and want.

Don't ever give up hope. Miracles happen every day and succe can come in the next moment.

Enjoy life today. Yesterday is past and tomorrow is y to happen.

It is the same in our journey to truth. That essential emptine that we come into this journey with, the emptiness that exis in the cup, is something that we should make strong an always carry. As you go through your practice, as you perfor your *sadhana* (spiritual effort), as you perform the spiritu routine of your daily life, keep a certain thirst within yoursel prayer must go on within you all the time, "Oh God, I want you. Oh God, I want you. Please come to me." That emptiness must not go away. That yearning must never fade or falter, that seeking must never disappear, right up until God comes to fulfil it.

☆ Don't ever give up hope. Miracles happen every day and success can come in the next moment ☆

You must, at all times, be aware of the fact that the journey is of utmost significance here. Umberto Eco wrote in *Foucault's Pendulum*: "But the important thing is not the finding, it is the seeking, it is the devotion with which one spins the wheel of prayer and scripture, discovering the truth little by little. If this machine gave you the truth immediately, you would not recognise it, because your heart would not have been purified by the long quest."

So be prepared for hard work and a lot of spiritual practice from your side. Making yourself empty is not as easy as it sounds. But you have to be empty in order to be enlightened. Remember, you can pour only as much tea into the cup as the emptiness that exists. Not more!

So if you make yourself empty of your own desperate clinging to your identity, if you can create some space within yourself for receiving divinity, then you shall have it. As a Sufi Master once said to his eager student, "Either you exist in you, or God exists in you. The both of you can't exist together."

An enlightened person knows that God exists in the space within is the reason why I often describe ego (our sense of separate identity) simply as an attempt to Edge God Out!

Our entire spiritual effort and practice; whatever we do to grow our awareness in our inner journey, whether it be yoga, prayer or meditation, is aimed to create that space within our self. To create emptiness, so that the divinity that is all around us can come into us.

Believe me, divinity is not limited to one person, one scripture, one religion or one place. God is too big to fit into any one religion.

Divinity is everywhere and in everything, all the time. It has always been so and it is so now as well.

Consider the phrase "God is NO-WHERE". Look at it again and realise it says, "God is NOW-HERE".

All it needs is a change of perspective.

You can have the experience right now, in this moment; it is just a matter of shifting your perspective. You can either find God in everyone and everything around you right now, or see divinity no-where. It is up to you.

Also keep in mind that though enlightenment can happen in flash, you should be in no rush to experience it.

Here is an interesting conversation chanced upon when browsing the internet:

Q: What does a Zen monk say to a hot dog stand vendor?

A: Make me one with everything.

Q: What does the vendor say when the monk asks for change for his twenty dollar bill?

A: Change comes from within.

☆ Divinity is not limited to one person, one scripture, one religion or one place. God is too big to fit into any one religion ☆

Jokes apart, there is a lesson for all of us in the above dialogue. If you want to be one with everything and everyone, much like a Zen monk, you have to change. Do not expect the externals to bring about your change. It has to come from deep within. You have to change your thoughts, your way of life and living. Only then will you be one with the universe.

Tip 2

Stay Empty

An enlightened person knows that
God exists in the space within

Chapter Three

Believe!

The real meaning of enlightenment is to gaze with undimmed eyes on all darkness.

Nikos Kazantzakis

Do you think God is beneficent to you or do you think God is against you?

This was one of the first questions that my spiritual Master asked me when I started on the journey to my own self. The question is important because the answer is the guiding force for all the steps that follow.

This is one of the most important and basic questions that we all must answer for ourselves when we set out on the spiritual path. The direction of our future spiritual practice depends on our answer.

If your answer is that God is beneficent to us, if the universe is for us, if my Creator is for me, then you must also logically ask, "Why would God create obstacles in my path? If my Creator is for me and I am walking towards Him or Her, then won't I get help to arrive there?"

This belief is critically important because if you have this perspective as you walk the path to your higher self, if you carry this outlook of life in every moment—that God is for me, S/He is helping me and I am walking towards God—then everything that follows in your life just becomes another signal or a pointer to where God is.

> ☆ If you have surrendered to your Creator, if you are convinced that you never walk alone, then you truly believe ☆

Please think a little deeply on this.

I am talking about a moment-to-moment attitude; something that is an intrinsic part of your inner awareness all the time. I want you to pause here and reflect. If you have surrendered to your Creator, if you are always motivated by your belief in God, if you are convinced that you never walk alone, then you truly *believe*.

But don't many of us leave this true belief for those days when everything is going wrong? Do we connect with our Maker only when we feel incapable of carrying on? Do we turn to God only during our days of stress and distress? Is God someone to be approached only when times are bad?

There are just two ways to live. One is that you feel that life is going to support you and the other is that you feel you have to struggle against it. There is no other way. For enlightenment to happen, you have to be convinced that God is with you, all-ways and at all times.

Most of us shift between these two extremes at different poin
in time. But essentially, these are the only two ways; either, th
universe is beneficial for me, it is going to support me, or, I ar
going to struggle against it to make out of it what I want, t
make out a living, to seek out my life. These are the only two a
titudes with which you can live your life.

But out of these two, if you believe that God is for you; that S/H
supports you in whatever you do, then you find that once yo
have embarked on your spiritual journey, secure in the beli
that it is God who is calling the shots, every moment, everythin
and everyone, will become another message, another signa
another lesson and another step closer to the final goal—th
experience of the ultimate. It is this simple truth that will s
you free.

Whether it be a person who gets on your nerves, an element
your discipline that you cannot stick to, a command from you
Master that you cannot obey, or a test that you fail to pass, a
of it just points you to where God is, to where your lesson li
and the areas where you have to work at yourself.

As you walk the path to the final goal, it is wise and helpful
remember, God is always for you, with you. S/He is beneficer
to you.

God helps you to come closer to yourself. God makes it eas
not difficult, for you to see the real you.

All difficulties are nothing but a lesson you have to learn about yourself, an obstacle you have to cross.

Well begun is half done is an old truth. By beginning in this positive manner, where you feel that every step is a guidance to your ultimate destination, you literally pull to yourself all that you need to progress speedily toward your goal.

☆ As you walk the path to the final goal, it is wise and helpful to remember, God is always for you, with you. ☆

Once you start to believe that all that happens is God's wish and guidance for you, you begin to learn lessons from everything and everyone. This is a spiritual secret, the alchemy that converts everything ordinary in your life to the extraordinary, everything normal to something mystical. You just have to learn to surrender to a higher power.

The first decision you make about the perspective you carry sets the direction for all your steps that follow.

Everything in life becomes easier once you have this perspective. To carry this perspective is up to *you*. It is not up to anybody else. This belief has its origin deep inside you. It is, in a sense, your greatest treasure.

For a person with belief can not only climb mountains he or she can reach great spiritual heights.

Convinced that you are a child of God and that your Creator
with you always, you can see light, everywhere.

When you carry the thought of God with you at all times, yo
see this light that drives you to the pinnacle of perfection.

This is the place where all spiritual seekers want to arriv
For this is where all boundaries get blurred; where all of u
unite to become one with our source. This is where all childre
of God are meant to reach. It is our journey and ou
destination; our path as well as our goal. It is where our so
dwells with the Creator.

As Marianne Williamson observed in *A Return to Love*: "Ou
deepest fear is not that we are inadequate. Our deepest fear
that we are powerful beyond measure. It is our light, not ou
darkness, that most frightens us. We ask ourselves, Who am I
be brilliant, gorgeous, talented, fabulous?

Actually, who are you not to be? You are a child of God. You
playing small doesn't serve the world. There's nothin
enlightened about shrinking so that other people won't fe
insecure around you.

We are all meant to shine, as children do. We were born t
manifest the glory of God that is within us. It's not just i
some of us; it's in everyone. And as we let our own light shin
we unconsciously give other people permission to do the sam

as we're liberated from our own fear, our presence automatically liberates others."

Enlightenment is a collective state of existence. It is good that your Master has seen the light and through the wise one's teachings, so have you.

> ☆ The goal is to enlighten everyone; the endeavour should be to take everyone along on the road to enlightenment ☆

But the goal is to enlighten everyone; the endeavour should be, at all times, to take everyone, your friends and family, your colleagues as well as your neighbours, along on the road to enlightenment.

We all have to see the light; in fact, we have to see beyond the light and realise that we are all one. That is what true enlightenment really is—you look at the 'stranger' sitting next to you and see none other than yourself. In him or her, you get a glimpse of yourself.

The Master decides to give his rapt student an important lesson. He calls him over and says, "Ignore these words of mine at your own peril. They can take you all the way to enlightenment, or they can keep you in darkness for centuries, the choice is yours. If you wish to understand that which is always with you, listen to me carefully now as I describe your eternal companion."

The boy sits at the Master's feet and listens carefully.

This is what his Master has to say:

Our Constant Companion

I am your constant companion.

I can be your greatest helper, or your heaviest burden, for I a
always with you in your life.

I can propel you to extraordinary success, or drag you down
miserable failure. I can be completely at your command. Mo
of the things you struggle to do, you might as well turn over
me, and I will do them quickly and correctly.

I am the servant of all great men. Those who are great, I ha
made them great. Those who are failures, I have made the
failures. I am not a machine, though I work with the precisio
of one. You may use me for profit or for ruin—it makes no di
ference to me.

Take me, accept me, train me, understand me, and I will plac
the world at your feet. Disregard me, or ignore me, and I wi
destroy you.

You know who I am. I have been with you forever. I am you
best friend, or your worst enemy.

I am your mind!

t is the mind that takes us to places
itherto unexplored. It takes us to
he realm of belief; it also leads us
o the world of despair, disbelief and
isaster.

Again, it is the mind that, once
tilled, takes us to our Creator.

t is, indeed, our best companion,
our greatest ally in our journey towards attaining
nlightenment, for it teaches us to believe.

☆ It is the mind that takes us to places hitherto unexplored. It takes us to the realm of belief; it also leads us to the world of despair, disbelief and disaster ☆

Tip 3

Trust in a higher power

A believer lives by the truth,
'God is for me, never against me'

Chapter Four

Accept Responsibility

He, knowing all, becomes the All.

Upanishad

I am sure that you have read a lot and possibly even heard
lot about the Master-disciple relationship; about the roles
each of them. The question you have to ask yourself is thi
"Who is more responsible for the disciple's growth? Does tha
responsibility lie with the Master or with the student? Does th
Master make sure that the student evolves, or is it in the hand
of the disciple?"

In the roles that they both play, the Master naturally gives an
the disciple receives. So who is responsible for the movemer
forward?

The answer is simple. As a disciple, you must accept th
responsibility of your own growth. You must believe and totall
live by the fact that your progress and your evolution is in you
own hands and no one else's, not even in the hands of you
Master. By doing this you take full responsibility for your li
and the Master just becomes a catalyst for your flowering
Needless to say, this does not diminish or in any way take awa
from the identity and value of the teacher, it simply makes hir
or her the key that is able to unlock you.

The disciple, not the Master, is responsible for the spiritual growth of the disciple. There has been many a weak and lazy disciple who has blamed the Master for his or her own failure, but on the spiritual path there is no such thing as a bad Master, there is only the ignorant disciple.

☆ It is up to the disciples to make the Master guide them to the experience of God ☆

to accept responsibility. It is up to the disciples to make the Master guide them to the experience of God. This is the truth that we as aspirants do not like to face, as it puts the responsibility of our own success upon us. We would much rather pass the buck. We fail to understand that to take full responsibility for our life is in itself a deeply spiritual act.

Let me tell you a small story from the ancient Indian epic, the Mahabharata. In this book, there is a character called Drona, who is the teacher of the princes of a certain kingdom, the largest and most powerful in India at that time. Drona is a teacher of the martial arts and is the most proficient one of his day. He is also a very strict man and has taken certain vows and made many promises to the king. One of the promises is that he will teach only the princes and nobody else, so that the techniques and knowledge that he imparts to them are not known to any other human being, who in the future may become an enemy of the kingdom. Thus the princes always remain above all others.

However, there is a tribal boy named Ekalavya who is eager to learn the warrior arts from Drona, for he rightly recognizes him as the best teacher.

One day he goes to Drona, pays him the proper tribute and asks, "Master, please teach me."

Drona finds out that the boy comes from a low class, from the hunter tribe, and, therefore, bound by his promise, refuses, "I cannot teach you because I have taken a vow only to teach the princes. Go away."

Ekalavya goes back very disappointed and dejected. But he does not give up. He goes into the forest and prays. The very purpose of his life was to learn from Drona and now Drona has refused him. What is he to do?

Then Ekalavya decides. He goes further into the forest, takes the clay from the banks of a flowing river and builds an image of Drona. Once the image of Drona is ready in the middle of the forest, he bows down before it and prays to Drona from the deepest part of his heart, saying aloud: "From today you are my teacher. I shall stand here before you and learn. Please teach me."

And what does he do after this heartfelt prayer? He stands up, makes himself a bow and an arrow, primes it to shoot and then waits.

He simply waits. His prayer has been so complete that he totally believes that whatever comes to him instinctively is now a message from his guru.

Whatever comes to him in his inner self, as inspiration, he simply accepts and follows. "Shoot here, shoot there, do this, do that, pull more, pull less, aim high, aim low"—Ekalavya follows exactly the instructions that come to him in his mind. And over a period of time, he learns the art of archery.

> ☆ The disciple knows that the guru is a part of God, a part that teaches you to take you back to Him ☆

A few years later, the young princes who have been learning from Drona are walking through the forest and they come across a dog barking incessantly. It becomes very irritating for them to listen to this continuous bark. The prince, Arjuna, one of the greatest archers of all time, takes out his bow and arrow and decides to shoot the dog the next time it barks.

The dog does start to bark again but before Arjuna can react, somebody else from the middle of the forest shoots five arrows into the mouth of the dog, so that his mouth is wedged open and cannot close. Thus, the barking stops.

When Arjuna sees this, he is scared, angry and dumbfounded —all at the same time! He is absolutely shocked because this is something that he is still not capable of. He is not proficient enough to do this. He tries to find out who has performed suc[h] an incredible act of skill. He walks into the forest and eventual[ly] meets Ekalavya and straightaway asks him, "Who is you[r] teacher?"

To this, Ekalavya replies, "Drona."

Hearing this, Arjuna gets really angry. He runs back to Dron[a] saying, "You've broken your promise to me."

Drona asks, "How do you say that?" Arjuna recounts th[e] incident and that Ekalavya told him that Drona is his teacher[.]

Drona walks with Arjuna into the forest to meet Ekalavy[a.] When he sees Ekalavya, Drona recognises him and says, "B[ut] I have never taught you. I refused to teach you, this I clearl[y] remember."

Ekalavya replies, "Yes Master, you did refuse to teach me, b[ut] I went into the forest and refused to give up on my deepe[r] driving desire." He then goes on to narrate for Dron[a] everything that followed.

Listening to the story of this young boy's unwaverin[g] determination, Drona asks him to show the skills that he ha[s] acquired. Ekalavya demonstrates for him all that he has learn[t.] Drona then realises that Ekalavya has learnt much more than h[e] has ever taught Arjuna, his favourite disciple.

The lesson from this story is that when the disciple is determined and is propelled by his desire to achieve something and is also ready to take all responsibility towards the final attainment of his goal, even the Master is helpless. He is forced to give him the teaching. And if the guru cannot do so, the disciple will nonetheless arrive at his goal for he is persistent and believes that the universe will provide for him. The disciple knows that the guru is a part of God, a part that teaches you to take you back to Him. And that guru, that essence, is all around you, all the time.

Guidance is available to you every moment. You just have to make yourself ready and then you will receive it

Guidance is available to you every moment. You just have to make yourself ready and then you will receive it. Not before that. Remember it has been said for centuries, "When the student is ready, the Master appears." You can also believe this as, "When the soil is prepared, the seed will arrive."

Some faiths say that once you come into the grace of a Master, you do not have to do anything else. All is already done. Be free! They tell you, this is where your karma has brought you and now you are not responsible for your actions, the Master will do everything.

Such teachings simply encourage the students to abdicate responsibility of their life rather than accepting it. It will never work like that. Even if you are with your spiritual Master, you own actions and perspectives, your own outlook, makes a lot of difference to your progress.

Do not throw the responsibility on the Master; it is yours to hold. You are still in charge of your actions, efforts, discipline, perseverance and perspective.

There were two brothers who would go and listen to the Buddha almost every day. Only one of those brothers was completely transformed over the years. People who knew the family remarked that he was now a whole new human being. But what about the other one, they asked? Why had he not changed? Surely the Buddha is lacking in something.

So one of these relatives goes to the Buddha and asks, "O Great Master, both these boys came to you regularly. How is it that one has been transformed and the other still remains the same?"

The Buddha replies, "One of them is open to me and the other closed."

A deep and profound truth simply stated. One is open, the other is closed. The motivation that we come with is our own.

All of you who are reading this book are doing so for different reasons. Each of you has a different background, a different ife, a different desire, even a different degree of desire, and you will all progress at different paces. But it is all up to *you*.

☆At every human being's door opportunity comes at some time or another, but you have to be awake enough to hear it ☆

If you are not open, if you are not receptive, even when the Master says something to you, it shall pass you by. You shall not understand its importance, nor give it the proper time and attention it deserves. Also, if you are simply going to pass the buck, without accepting the fact that the buck stops with you, you are never going to proceed in your journey towards enlightenment.

The student is like the soil that accepts the seed that is thrown upon it. The seed may be good and have all the potential to sprout contained within it, but if the soil is not prepared and ready to hold it, the seed cannot be blamed.

The student is the soil, the Master throws the seed. The soil must make itself ready to receive, to hold and to nurture and cherish the seed, for flowering to take place.

In the business world, one is taught that opportunity always knocks on your door. At every human being's door opportunity comes at some time or another, but you have to be awake enough to hear it. Otherwise, opportunity knocks, nobody opens the door and it moves on to the next house.

When the knock comes, to be able to hear it and open the door is your responsibility. This is where your discipline and spiritual practice help you. When the Master says something to be able to accept and follow it is your responsibility. To be able to create that emptiness within yourself is your *sadhana*. To be accepting and receptive is your spiritual discipline.

To be able to surrender yourself because that is the only way you are going to be open, is your *sadhana*; to be able to give up and let go of some of the things that you hold on to so dearly is your spiritual endeavour.

It is so easy to play the blame game. We have all done it at some time or the other. But keep in mind that this is your personal growth, your spiritual evolution that you are dealing with here. The stakes are very high for the reward is huge. Enlightenment does not come easy. Accept that and work towards attaining that state of bliss where you connect with your Creator.

Be spiritually aware at all times. Throughout human history and culture, selected individuals from different walks of life have cultivated the ability to live life in a spiritual way, perceiving depths to which others were blind, and expressing love in ways that most of us have seldom seen.

These are people who have accepted fully the truth that they are not going to live forever and have made a choice ased on this acceptance—they have decided to live life fully, in each and every moment.

> ☆ Enlightenment does not come easy. Accept that and work towards attaining that state of bliss where you connect with your Creator ☆

These are people who have learnt to live from the heart, rather than to dwell in the mind.

They have made a choice to express, give and share their love, thereby holding nothing inside, and as a result remaining empty to receive.

They have a life based on total faith, rather than on pure logic.

These people have understood that faith is what your heart tells you is true even when your mind cannot prove it.

They live by the truth that we are not human beings having a spiritual experience; rather, spiritual beings having a physical one. They have clearly seen the destination of the journey we are on and thereby do not spend time and energy gathering possessions that they will eventually be forced to leave behind. They have learnt to live a life of awareness.

Seeing the awareness with which such people lead their lives shows us the way we can make ourselves healthier, happier and holier, letting go of illusions and awakening to the truth behind them.

Some of the common characteristics of those who are spiritual
aware are:

Trait 1: *Appreciating the gifts*
They see clearly the many gifts that the universe provides us i
every experience and in every person. They carry this vision i
every moment to such an extent that their first response is t
look for the good and the positive in everything, even in th
most negative of events or the worst of people.

Trait 2: *Fullness of experience*
They go into everything deeply, fully and totally, withou
holding themselves back once they have decided what they wan
to do. This total giving is actually a form of surrender in whic
they give all their mental, emotional, physical and spiritua
energies into the act of the moment. This total giving c
themselves creates an emptiness within, which allows them t
experience each experience in its fullness in a manner other
never do.

Trait 3: *Belief in action (karma)*
Invariably all elevated spirits believe in being mediums c
instruments of action. They are conscious of their roles a
creators and they create willingly and knowingly. They als
demonstrate largeness of vision. They clearly understand an
believe in the counsel of the Dhammapada: "However man
words you read, however many you speak, what good will the
do if you do not act upon them?" They are people of action an

inspire others to create—through action. However, action is not synonymous with struggle in their awareness.

Trait 4: *Exercise choice of attitude*

They know that the choice of how they want to react to a happening, any happening, is up to them. They are the

☆ Be spiritually aware at all times ☆

masters of their own attitude to life and everything in it. They choose to act, rather than to react, to stimulus of different kinds in their life. They create the happiness or the unhappiness in their life.

Trait 5: *Love is the basis of living*

Such people are consciously aware of the effect and resultant power of performed actions and spoken words. Therefore, they base their life on the bedrock of love and compassion, which is transmitted through their thoughts, words and deeds, to all around them. Even a harsh word or action, at times, is motivated by the greater good of the individual and originates in their compassion and caring.

For them, love is the key that opens all hearts. As Dr M Scott Peck rightly put it, "Nirvana or lasting enlightenment or true spiritual growth can be achieved only through the persistent exercise of real love."

The emphasis is on real, unconditional love that empowers the giver and the receiver. It is the highest form of love.

Trait 6: *Recognise, accept and let go*
Such people keenly recognise the opportunity for sel
expression and self-evolution that every moment and ever
choice brings before them. Understanding the futility c
resistance or rejection, they gracefully accept whatever th
moment brings to them, utilise it based on their self-awarenes
and as gracefully let go when it inevitably happens. In a
moments, they remain open and free.

Trait 7: *Accept death as an inevitable transition*
Such people do not think themselves to be invincible, everlas
ing or permanent. They are acutely aware of the eternal NOV
and the impermanence of all other forms of illusion. The
therefore, accept the reality that they, too, will one day have t
change—passing through the transition we call death. Instea
of facing this with the emotion of fear, they choose to embrac
it with gratitude and interest, as if meeting a long-lost friend. A
a result of this wholesome attitude, they value time and expres
no value for hurry, rush or impatience in daily tasks.

The disciple has been progressing well and is summoned fc
another important lesson in the ways of the wise.

"Hear the eternal good news about your own life today," say
the Master to the boy: "The good news, eternally, is that an
bad news can be turned into good news...if only we change ou
attitude!

We can be sad because the roses have thorns...or we can celebrate because the thorns have beautiful roses.

We can spend our life looking at all that we do not have, or we can be blissful by looking at all that we do have.

We can count our blessings or we can count our problems.

The eternal good news is that happiness or misery is decided by our attitude...and our attitude can be decided by us."

☆ You alone are responsible for your present state ☆

t is all in the mind—in *your* mind. There is no doubt about his. You alone are responsible for your present state. If you vant to live in a state of enlightenment, it is only you who are reating the barriers that are preventing you from arriving here. Your mind is demarcating the boundaries; your inner elf is defining the obstacles. Free yourself from all these blocks nd see your spirit soar.

Tip 4

Be persistent

Aspirants know that they alone are responsible for their enlightenment

Chapter Five

Light the Fire

Education is not the filling of a pail, but the lighting of a fire.

William Butler Yeats

There is a great difference between the religions of today and what true spirituality is. All religions are good as a belief system to live your life upon. They must, however, also teach you to offer that freedom that you have, without prejudice, to others.

Spirituality is a different ball game altogether. Spirituality about your own spirit and its origin with God. Spirituality about knowing and remembering your own truth.

To be spiritual you do not necessarily need religion. You need spiritual knowledge; you need a path to know your real self, to arrive at the personal experience of who you really are. As I have said earlier, all religions are good as belief systems, but it is also essential to understand that all religions have originated around spiritual people who were not religious (as they were labelled in their time for rebelling against the existing beliefs).

Because Christ was, so Christianity happened. Because the Buddha was, so Buddhism happened.

But, when Jesus Christ was there, what did he teach? He said, "Simply follow me. Believe in what I say, do what I tell you to do and I will take you to the final destination." He did not ask us to follow ten, twenty, thirty, forty different laws or ten, twenty, thirty, forty different labels and churches.

The same is true for the Buddha and Buddhism. All the great and enlightened teachers emphasised the fact that the journey is all about the discovery of the spirit within every human being. They did not proclaim to give something that did not already exist within the seeker. The Masters merely changed the perspective of the aspirant, changed his or her eyes, so to say, to allow the truth to shine through.

☆ All the great and enlightened teachers emphasized the fact that the journey is all about the discovery of the spirit within every human being ☆

Go into your inner being, they guided thousands of years ago; exactly the same thing that we learn today: Go within yourself. There is no new truth in this world, all truth is old. That is why it is called the truth, because it has always existed and will always exist, long after you and I have gone.

There is no new truth that the real Masters are here to give; every Master just presents the old truth in a new way. And if any Master claims to have come across some new truth that has never before been known, that Master is no Master at all.

All the religions of this world teach you how to live in a proper way, according to them. 'According to them' is the key phrase here, so if you really want to discover the truth, even their way must be questioned.

One good thing though is that no matter what the religion, teaches you how to live in peace with society. This, however, does not necessarily mean that you become aware of your spirit or you grow in a spiritual way. Religion and spirituality are like the banana peel and the fruit within. You buy the fruit so you can peel the banana for the fruit within, not for the peel itself!

In a similar fashion, you follow a religion to arrive at the core of spirituality within it, not to remain stuck at the external level of the religion and its traditions alone. The peel does have its own purpose but the real goal is the fruit within. That is what you want to eat, not the peel.

Let me now bring you to a very interesting truth. If you see a dry log before you, you will realise that this dry wood can catch fire only if you take the fire from somewhere else and bring it to touch the wood. Correct? The dry log will then, and only then, catch fire. It will not burn till the fire, which is already lit, is brought to touch it. If you want to understand how enlightenment happens, ask where the fire exists originally. Is it inside the wood or is it outside it? Think deeply.

Consider again, carefully, with full awareness. There is a piece of dry wood. And you know it can catch fire only if you bring fire from outside and touch it. But where is the fire available or living? Is it inside that piece of wood that you hold or is it outside? The answer is that it is in both places! It is inside the wood or the wood would not catch fire. And it is also outside the wood because you can see it and feel it clearly and, without that, the wood will not catch fire in the first place.

Similarly, God is already inside you and God is in the Master as well. The difference between you and a real Master is that in the Master the experience of divinity is alive, it is real. In the Master the fire is burning already while yours is still to be lit. The fire that is in the Master needs to reach out and touch the fire within you. And then transformation happens.

☆ Only when you dissolve and merge with the higher power, will you become both, annihilated as well as enlightened ☆

The fire is in you, in the Master, and God is the fire itself! And all three are seeking each other to merge. When these three become one, the fire burns bright. That's how enlightenment happens. The trinity becomes one.

And only when you dissolve and merge with the higher power, will you become both, annihilated as well as enlightened. You, as you know yourself or as your family or friends know you, will no longer exist. Instead, there will be a higher version of your own self, minus the ego and a sense of the self. The 'I' in you will be gone. You will see the universe with new eyes. Nothing will be the same. In fact, you may have the sensation of being outside of your body. This is a great feeling and this is what we are all working towards. To unite with our Creator, to realise that we are all indeed one for our source is the same. You will be spiritually aware, all the time.

Awareness is the practice of staying awake moment to moment; to be fully present and available to the moment, moment after moment; to be totally conscious and mindful. Creating this state of awareness is the first step towards the ability to change your life and destiny. The more aware you become of being aware, the greater your ability grows and vice versa.

I have listed here twenty-five ways in which your awareness in the moment can transform each challenging moment into a new and true beginning for you. Learning to be aware in these moments leads to authentic inner change, which is synonymous with being in charge of your own destiny.

It is essential to remember that as you awaken to the higher awareness within yourself, you naturally attract to yourself happier and higher events and opportunities for change. As the ancient Masters and holy scriptures of all cultures repeatedly remind us, there is no such thing as a wasted step when your final destination is mastery of the self.

. Step out of the race and into your own life

Awareness cannot come where a mad race is being run after a seemingly elusive goal. Dare to slow down your life and step out of the rush to do more and more, possess more and more.

No matter how fast your thoughts and desires run, they finally take you nowhere. To find the timeless, dare to step out of the daily grind of chasing time. Live as though you have all the time in the world at your command and can truly decide how to use it.

> ☆ Awareness is the practice of staying awake moment to moment; to be fully present and available to the moment ☆

. Accept responsibility of your life-experience and everything in it

Whatever you experience in your life, that is, whatever happens in your life, and the way you feel and react towards it, is a direct expression of who you are. At the deepest level, everything occurring in your life-experience is the result of your own desires, choices, actions and reactions.

Therefore, accept full responsibility and, thereby, the control of your own life—control both of what your life is now, and what you want it to be.

. Release all resentments and blame

If you truly accept responsibility for your life, and believe in a higher order in which things function, you spontaneously

release all blame and resentments. It is important for you to se
that holding on to some hurt or hatred over what others ma
have done in the past makes you their slave in the present mc
ment, in the here and now.

4. Refuse to have a short-term vision
Simply drop any desire, thought or action that promises shor
term, temporary or instant gratification but results in a moi
permanent conflict or disharmony.

Simply choose to be whole. Begin by consciously refusing t
compromise yourself.

5. Go beyond the best you think you are, or can do
Anyone in life can do what everyone else does, which is nothin
extraordinary. Do more than you think you can; take the ste
you think you cannot.

Dare to leave security and comfort behind. The limits you hav
known are the ones you are secure and comfortable witl
The ones you still have to explore are the ones that make yo
insecure and uncomfortable. See this. Then start going beyon
your known self.

6. Give up judgements
The easiest and most unconscious thing to do is to walk aroun
judging every moment, event and person who comes int
your life. Remember that even when you judge, you do s

from your own level of awareness, and if you want to raise that, you must turn your attention to yourself, inwards, not outwards towards others.

If you give up passing judgement on all, you will be a lot more tolerant and a lot more ready to accept a whole lot of things. This is how Wayne Dyer defines enlightenment: "the quiet acceptance of what is".

☆ Choose to be whole. Begin by consciously refusing to compromise yourself ☆

7. Lighten up

The heart feels heavy when every thought and emotion is taken seriously, as a permanent reality. Keep in mind that your true nature is neither thought nor emotion, rather a pure, free and light spirit. Look at every moment of life through its eyes.

8. Face your own fears

There is really no such thing as external fear. All of it exists only within you, as a result of one or the other reason. So the next time you start to feel fear, don't look outside you for the reason, instead look inwards. It is the inner ground you are standing on that isn't stable. Any fear or weakness faced by looking in this new direction becomes the foundation of a new strength. Fear comes, face it.

Fearlessness follows!

9. Understand interdependence and inter-connectedness

There is no such thing as separate selves. In reality, there is onl
one. We are all part of one consciousness, one universe. W
make up one song. We all are in harmony with our Maker. S
anything you do for another that leads to betterment in any wa
also results in the same for you. Try a little kindness, or hel
others, even if you are not feeling that way at the moment. Yo
will find yourself feeling better. Give yourself a boost, by givin
it to others.

10. Do what is right regardless of consequences

To choose, and do, what's right for you, in spite of fearing th
consequences that choice may bring is the same as giving your
self a fearless life. What you are afraid of losing can never be th
source of your fearlessness.

Do what's right, regardless of the fear or the consequences. A
you can finally lose is your fear. And fear is something you t
lose, sooner rather than later, as you walk the path towards en
lightenment.

11. Stop explaining yourself to seek understanding

The only reason for always ensuring that others are happy wit
you or for the need to endlessly explain your life to others i
that you seek justification of who you are in the other's eye:
You seek the confirmation of your identity from the lives of oth
ers. At a deeper level, this arises from a feeling of insecurit
within yourself.

2. Realise that the emptiness needs to fill itself

You have tried in countless ways: through relationships, ego expressions and possessions, to fill the emptiness within. It has never worked; the emptiness remains. Stop trying so desperately to fill up the space and

☆ We are all part of one consciousness, one universe. We make up one song ☆

leave it empty. This allows the emptiness to eventually fill itself. And, remember, being empty is essential if you want to be enlightened.

3. Understand interdependence and inter-connectedness

Put what you love first, above all. The rest of your life will take care of itself once you do this because true love always finds a way.

Love never considers fear. And with love as your guiding light, your success in life is assured because even in work, when you do what you love, you have tremendous interest and enjoyment. Love is what makes the world tick; it is also your strongest ally on the road to enlightenment.

4. Understand interdependence and inter-connectedness

It is a fact that defeat is only a perception from a small vision. It has no real life of its own except what you give it. This means that the only time you have to feel the pain of any defeat is if you ask for it—by delving into troubled thoughts about some painful past loss. Any so-called defeat is also only temporary,

unless you make it permanent in your consciousness. Stay i
the present moment. Consciousness likes great heights; dar
to follow!

15. Start all over again if neccessary

Any time you truly choose, you can start your life all over agair
without permission from any higher authority. You can have ju
as many new beginnings as you are willing to leave behind all o
your old ideas and conditioning about right and wrong. Lif
can be as new as you choose it to be.

16. Stop looking outside of yourself

After endlessly looking for it outside, realise that the answer i
within you. Your life is only as complete as you are—no more
no less. Looking to your work, relationships or events for a fee
ing of self-completion is a self-defeating exercise. Being com
plete and whole is first an understanding, and then a state o
being. Completion does not need a certain set of conditions t
be perfectly manifested for its occurrence.

17. Remember there is a divine order

The raindrop needs the ocean, just as the ocean needs the rain
drop. The river runs to the sea because each stream finds an
fills its own course. The universe renews and replenishes itsel
because there is a divine intelligent order to all things. Kee
this in mind in each moment of each day, regardless of what i
happening around you or to you. Go with the flow of the uni
verse.

8. Let go

Trying to control every moment of our life, or another's, causes more disharmony than any other process. Everything and every person must go through their own lives, based on their own awareness, at their own pace. Allow this to happen.

✫ Stay in the present moment. Consciousness likes great heights; dare to follow ✫

Let something higher have its hand at directing your life. As they say, let go, let God.

9. Don't live for others

There is no satisfying the fear that you may displease others. Allowing what others may feel about what you want to do to change how you feel is like believing that someone else can live your life for you.

The only real strength comes from knowing that you have your own likes and dislikes in your life and can never make everyone happy with everything that you are, or can do.

20. Jump into action

Wisdom turns into strength only if it is followed up with action. To learn how to swim, you must first get wet. Any weakness voluntarily faced and met is the same as greeting a greater strength. Wisdom lays the foundation, but it is action that finally changes life and the future.

21. *Be optimistic*

You always have two choices in every situation—either curse the darkness, or light a candle. Choose the more positive attitude always. It comes at the same expense as the negative thought or choice but with extremely different consequences.

Why wait until you feel down before you think of looking up? You can always glimpse the higher, in every moment, but you have to remind yourself to look in the right direction. An enlightened soul is one who knows where to look. He or she knows what works because they invariably listen to their inner voice.

22. *Understand the difference between the head and the heart*

No matter how much you try, you can't think yourself into happiness. You must actually happy. However, you can sink yourself to your lowest low with a chain of thoughts that start from a single negative one.

Bright, positive emotions spring from the heart. Heavy feelings cannot exist without the presence of negative thoughts. This means that sad states are just a trick of the mind and begin with our thoughts.

23. *Enjoy silence*

The frantic search for an answer will only deliver an answer that originates in the same frantic level. Enjoy silence and do not consider it an enemy. It is okay to not know.

Knowing that you do not know, and accepting that fact, puts you where you need to be to learn. Just as one can see farther on a clear day, new wisdom flowers in silence and stillness.

✦ You can always glimpse the higher, in every moment, but you have to remind yourself to look in the right direction ✦

24. *Walk one step at a time*

Do not be too concerned about how much there is to do, or how impossible some of the tasks seem. Just get one thing done at a time, again and again. Just do what is in your power and brush aside all other concerns.

The journey of a thousand miles begins with a single step. And the most beautiful tapestry begins and ends with one of ten thousand individual threads.

25. *Know that the time is always 'now'*

You cannot change the mind of the person you are later. There is no later, it's always now or never. This moment, ever present, ever powerful, is before you. And it has limitless potential. The time to change your destiny is 'NOW'.

To conclude this chapter, here is another story of the wise Master and his eager student:

The Master calls the boy to him and says, "Today you must go to another teacher to learn."

"Where do I go, Master?" asks the boy.

The Master replies, "Even though you can learn about your ow
truth from everyone and everything around you, because Go
is everywhere, I think today you should go and learn from th
oyster. He is a great and wise teacher..."

So the boy goes off to the ocean, and this is the lesso
he learns.

Sometimes, things irritate the oyster. They get into his shel
into his comfort zone. And then he is no longer comfortab
or happy. He does not like them at all and tries to get ri
of them.

But, after all his struggle with his irritations, when he realize
that it does not work, he settles down to create one of the mos
beautiful things in the world from them.

He coats them, and coats them, till the irritation itself ha
become a beautiful shiny pearl.

The boy learns that even though there is irritation in ever
person's life, there is only one remedy when everything els
does not work—use the irritation to make yourself better, se
clearer, value correctly and seek the correct thing. You hav
to learn from the bad times; in fact, I strongly believe tha
bad times exist for only one purpose and that is to show u

he path that takes us directly to our
etter self. Embedded in each of us is
his precious pearl that is waiting to be
liscovered.

o let us hone our outer shells, the oys-
er if you will. Let us work patiently but
ersistently at trying to reach our
igher selves and connect with our Creator. Let us realise that
leep within us is this pearl that is our most valuable possession.

When you attain enlightenment, you will realise that this pearl
s all that matters in life. It is your soul and your sole reason to
e alive. Don't let it get obscured by irritation.

> ☆ You cannot change
> the mind of the
> person you are later.
> There is no later,
> it's always now
> or never ☆

Tip 5

Put yourself on fire

A seeker will always strive intensely
to improve from within

Chapter Six

Allow the Universe to Reflect You

One moon shows in every pool; in every pool, the one moon.

Zen saying

What do we value the most about ourselves? Just think about this question sincerely for a minute.

If you believe that whatever is valuable to us we hold on to tightly, then it would seem that the things we value the most are our own faults, mistakes and shortcomings.

How can I say that? Because we hold on to our faults and weaknesses so tightly, we just refuse to let them go. We don't even want the world or anyone else to see our deficiencies so we hold them close to our heart and protect them forever. We keep them hidden.

We talk so much about our good points, but do we talk about our problems? No, those we cannot share! If you consider that it is only those things that we consider valuable and precious that we do not want to give away, that we do not want to share, you will be amazed. You will come to the realisation that you have been holding on to the very thing that you should have let go. You have protected the very thing that has been keeping you down.

Those that we keep hidden are also those that we wish to be rid of—our faults, our mistakes and all our own problems. These are the things that bother us again and again throughout life. Yet we hold on to them so tightly, refusing to let anybody see them, touch them or share them.

☆ A very simple way of living in this world and yet being happy is simply to believe that everything happens due to God's will ☆

Therefore, our spiritual practice, or a part of it, is to open up and let go of things, thereby making space for something new to enter. We all know that our past life or our old life was not good enough for us and that is why we are here walking the path to something better, something more meaningful. Why can't we just let go of everything in our past, become a new human being, totally open, to be able to receive a whole new type of life, a whole new outlook, a whole new perspective?

A very simple way of living in this world and yet being happy regardless of what happens in our world is simply to believe that everything happens due to God's will. I know it is difficult to believe this when you have questions such as: Why do a hundred people die at a time? Why are there diseases such as cancer and AIDS?

But for a minute, let us take just the perspective of one human being, one individual.

You have two choices before you. The first is to believe that everything happens at random, by accident, and there is no order behind things. That there is no higher power, no intelligent consciousness, no God or divinity and nobody knows how these things happen. And yet they happen. And when they happen to you at random, you react to them. Based on how things happen to you, you have to take your action which is called a reaction.

The second choice that is open to you is to believe that there is a higher intelligence, there is consciousness, there is certain balance and reason in things and that there is God and divinity behind what's happening. Once you start to believe that, then life actually becomes very simple and easy because you feel that everything has a reason and purpose to manifest and you begin to look into that reason and purpose.

It is only when you begin to feel this way that you eventually arrive at the spiritual truth that you are the creator of your life through the instrument of action. Action that actually takes birth in your mind and simply matures and manifests in the physical world.

Initially one essential shift is required; that you change your perspective and start to accept that even if something bad is happening to you, perhaps it is bad only in the way you are looking at it. Maybe it is not as bad in the absolute sense.

Good and bad are your judgements after all, nothing else. What is bad from your human eyes may be good from the eyes of the universe. All that you call crisis is simply called a test from the eyes of another.

> ☆ The world is nothing but a mirror reflecting back to you what is inside you already ☆

If you change that outlook towards something, then that very thing by itself changes. There is a Hindi proverb that says if you change the way you look at things, only then does the entire creation change for you.

We agree that there is just one world in which we live and die. Yet this one world is different for each one of us because of how we perceive it. Internally our pictures of the world are different even though externally it is just one world. Thus the spiritual truth is that if you change that perception, if you change the way you look at it, then the entire world, the entire creation, changes for you.

The universe will reflect what you want to see.

In the ancient holy book, the Talmud, is a verse that states, "We see the world not as it is but as we are." Thus, as you keep changing, the world keeps changing for you. The world is nothing but a mirror reflecting back to you what is inside you already.

We are logical enough to understand that as we gro
spiritually, we start having different values, we start thinkin
of things differently and we start looking at the worl
differently. Yet, we all know, the world remains the sam
nothing changes in it. Neither does the world change, nor d
the people in it. What changes is only us, but that brings abou
a change in everything and everyone. It has happened n
because the externals have changed, but because the intern;
has changed.

It is a truth that the entire world is just a reflection of who yo
are. If you are a person who is full of fear inside, then this worl
will give you enough reason and opportunity for that fear t
come out. It is a reflection in the sense that it brings out wh;
you are. It verifies it; it justifies it. It makes your truth the trut
of this world. If you are a person full of love, then this worl
will give you enough opportunity for that love to come out an
be expressed.

Thus we arrive at the spiritual law—whatever you focu
on, grows!

However, do not forget that the world will only give you wha
you already are. It all depends on who you are because th
world by itself is very neutral. It is quite like a handgun. Is
handgun good or bad? The fact is that it is neither. It is just
handgun. It is neutral. You give it into the hands of someon
who has criminal intent and it becomes bad—a tool fo

destruction. And you give it into the hands of someone who has a noble task and it becomes good—a tool for protection. The holder gives it its inherent quality.

☆ The quest for our highest self is an inner game. It is not about the external world ☆

The world is just like that. It is simply a reflection of who we are. We all have a certain impression of the world that we live in. What is important is to realise that actually our impression of the world, or our ideas on the existence of consciousness, divinity or God, are such because, in truth, we are like that.

We make the world what it is. To change the world or people around us, we must change ourselves first and then the world around us will change, too.

So keep this very clear in your mind. The quest for our highest self is an inner game. It is not about the external world. It is about changing yourself, not about changing others. It is not about outer pretences. It is not about looking different, being different, feeling different or showing the whole world that you are a different human being. It does not matter how you look. It does not matter what you do. What matters is what is happening inside you.

And that makes all the difference. If the inner changes, then everything outside changes as well.

Your spiritual discipline and practice is only for changing you it is not for changing the world. Change yourself first and then work with others. These are some basic principles that w forget when we commence on the spiritual path—this inne game. Do not play this game outside of yourself. Do not star collecting spiritual knowledge or equipment just becaus before this you have been collecting non-spiritual knowledg and equipment.

Before you started on the spiritual path, perhaps you wer collecting cars or relationships, and now you are collectin; spiritual knowledge, workshops or equipment. That is the onl difference! You have carried the habit of the outer world to th inner world, too. If the nature of the seeker has not changed the inner perspective of the person has not changed, the nothing has changed; no matter how many years he or she ha been on the path.

There is a very apt saying, "Wherever you go, there you are. There once was a man in a village in ancient India who wa always complaining. He felt that he was better than the rest c the villagers and that everyone else was completely stupid an illiterate as compared to him. One day, he decides to go to th spiritual Master in the village. He thinks, I should find out wha to do because I cannot live my life like this. I am getting to frustrated. So he visits the Master and says, "Master, I have big problem. This village gets on my nerves. Everybody here i so dumb. What should I do?"

The Master asks, "Well, do you know of any other village where people are up to your standards?"

"Yes Master," he replies at once. "There is a village across the mountains and I think the people here are very intelligent."

> ☆ You have to change what is inside you. Then everything around you will be different ☆

"Well, then go there," advises the wise Master. "Come back after six months and let me know if they are really as intelligent as you think they are."

The man goes and, six months later, he is back and guess what? He is still complaining. He says, "Master, I thought they were very intelligent, but you know they are just like these people here. I was stupid to go there."

The Master replies, "You were stupid to think in the first place that these people are stupid. Wherever you go, there you are. You are not changing what's inside you and that's the whole problem. Do not expect your world to change if you don't!"

So whether you go to a discotheque, a nightclub, a bar or to an ashram—wherever you go, there you are.

Whatever clothes and accessories you have on your body is not important. What you eat or drink, or don't eat and drink, is not important. What is important is how you are changing

within yourself, for that is the key to changing everythin
outside yourself. You have to change what is you. The
everything around you will be different. This is the whol
secret to transformation.

Change yourself and everything changes. Divinity has alway
been around you, inside you, outside you and in everything i
your life. You have not seen it yet not because it is not there bu
because you have been looking with the wrong eyes.

Change your eyes and God is everywhere. Keep the sam
eyes and God is nowhere. From the perspective of the ignoran
God is difficult to find; from the eyes of a Master, God i
impossible to miss.

And now to another delightful teaching story. The Master call
the boy to him and says, "There will soon come a time whe
you will go out into the world and people will seek you.

"They will come to learn from you. They will ask you to teac
them the mysteries of the universe, the secrets of the mind, eve
ask you to show them the light of God. They will ask for hap
piness, success and love from you. At such times, remember tha
most of them are only concerned with being happy on a dail
basis and living a life of comfort and security. So instead of giv
ing them high and difficult spiritual truths when they begi
their journey, give them a simple path to living a life of free
dom."

"How will I do that Master?" asks the boy.

Teach them these five principles, which, if followed, will ensure for them a life of happiness, freedom and joy: Teach them to keep their heart free from hate. Teach them to keep their mind free from worry. Teach them to live simply. Teach them to expect little from life and others. Teach them to give much to life and to others."

☆ Change your eyes and God is everywhere. Keep the same eyes and God is nowhere ☆

Spirituality is not something esoteric or difficult to understand and pursue. On the contrary, the way I see it, spirituality is a simple exercise. The path to enlightenment is paved with simple deeds, simple thoughts and simple practices. If you can reflect these, you are well on your way to reaching the divine. Give what you want to receive; realise that if the world has to change, it has to begin with one person and that one person is you. A single thought or act of yours can initiate a whole movement.

Think about that.

Tip 6

Seek enlightenment everywhere

The enlightened person knows that the world is a mirror

Chapter Seven

Take the Bite

By plucking her petals, you do not gather the beauty of the flower.

Rabindranath Tagore

Transformation is a game of awareness that we are playing. The moment you become totally aware of who you are in reality, the game is over; it stops. Now you have arrived and a new game begins.

In this game, the lowest level of existence is one where you do not even know what awareness means—you are not even aware about awareness itself. However, this is where we all start out from, and slowly grow, bit by bit.

The important thing here is that we have to evolve and we have to be ready to accept change. We have to be prepared to take our growth to the next level.

There are many techniques to bring about transformation within yourself, such as yoga and meditation. Prayer and chanting of mantras are others. Introspection, self-enquiry, contemplation, concentration, all of these are also means to go inwards within yourself. Any technique or means, which makes you more aware of how you behave, how you act, how you feel, how you emote and how you perceive, is a valid way.

t is said that there are as many ways to awareness as there are people on our planet. You just have to pick the way that is best suited for you. And then get ready to literally take the plunge. The means as well as the techniques are many, you could choose any one of them, but the key is to go into it very deeply. The final result of all techniques, though, is the same— total awareness. All paths lead you to the same destination when followed to the end.

☆ Introspection, self enquiry, contemplation, concentration, all of these are also means to go inwards within yourself ☆

Our problem sometimes is that we constantly try new paths without holding on to any one till the end. Thus, we never arrive at the destination; we constantly and forever stay on the path.

To stay on your chosen path to the very end, it is imperative that you incorporate the three Ds that I have mentioned earlier—Discipline, Devotion and Dedication—into your everyday spiritual practice.

Discipline is of the physical body. Devotion comes from the heart within and involves your feelings. Dedication is from the use of the mind.

Discipline says that you must do your practice at the prescribed time; you will not delay, procrastinate or abort for a seemingly good reason. Devotion says that you will put your heart and soul into the practice when you do it and will not allow it to be hollow. Dedication says that you will stick to it even when you feel like giving up or are feeling depressed because no result seems to be accruing. You will persevere till the very end.

Simple awareness is something very hard to achieve even though it sounds easy. To arrive at that simple awareness you need a lot of discipline and practice. It is not as if you can wake up one minute and say, "Oh God, now I am aware." Unfortunately, it never happens like that. You have to work a lot on yourself to be able to arrive at a stage where you are ready and only then can awareness come to you. You have to make the soil ready to receive the seed.

Realise that we have played two games simultaneously for many lifetimes. One, the game of living in this world and running after the accumulation of all the material rewards and comforts the world provides. Second, the game of seeking our real identity, our true self; searching for what we call divinity and God. We have been playing both these games in this lifetime as well. Thus, you have arrived in this existence with all the things you have collected and accumulated in your past—your mental impressions (or, as they are called in Sanskrit) of all your previous lives and existence.

And now the question that remains is this: What do you want to do with your life and existence?

To get the awareness of who you are in your original state in a total way is not an easy job because for many years, for many hundreds of years, you have been grabbing on to external, material things and believing them to be real. You have constantly and continuously been searching for security, identity, meaning and truth in the externals, so now it becomes extremely difficult to search within. In fact, it is extremely difficult even to reverse the flow of this direction, from external to internal, from without to within.

Understand that whenever the mind says or thinks something, you think what it is saying or thinking is you. Thus, when somebody opposes your thought or opinion, you feel hurt because you feel they are opposing you. You forget that it is only one thought or one opinion of yours out of the many thousands that you will have in just one day. If you have this realisation, you will remain calm and peacefully allow others to disagree with you without feeling or becoming any less.

☆ We have to do a lot of spiritual exercise just to free ourselves from the chains that have kept us bound for all these years without our knowing it ☆

If you cannot allow others to disagree with you without getting angry, it is only due to a deep sense of insecurity that exists within you. A sense of insecurity that clearly says that any disagreement with your thoughts and opinions will make you less than what you are. You feel that disagreement will threaten your identity. This is because you are not rooted deeply and firmly in your identity in the first place. Hence the insecurity.

Why identify with something that the mind has cropped up? It is as if you put on the DVD and then begin to think that you are actually in the movie. This is the nature of the mind; this is how the mind works. It creates a thought and you believe you are the thought itself. You are neither the movie, nor the thought. So, if somebody says it is a bad movie, why should it bother you? Or when somebody says that your thought is bad, it should not bother you. But without any awareness of who we are or how our mind works, we have been repeating this same pattern over and over again.

This is the same process by which a mantra works so effectively. Do you know what a mantra does when you repeat it again and again? By repeating it with your attention and awareness on it, you allow it to create a groove in your mind. You allow it to seep into your subconscious mind through reciting it consciously and continuously with your conscious mind. Once that is done, if ever you feel a bit shaky, or a crisis comes your way, your mind automatically goes back to that groove in which the mantra resides. This is how the mantra helps you.

Now, it does not take much intelligence to realise that we have been repeating another mantra, too, without even being aware of it. Because it has been constantly repeated, you now believe t to be your truth. The mantra that you have been repeating all the time is this, "My thought is me, my feeling is me, my emotion is me, my desire is me. My action is me, my position is me, my wealth is me, my power is me, my name is me, my fame is me, my possessions are me." These grooves are now very deep in your subconscious mind. Very, very deep! It is very difficult to eradicate them or go against them. This is the reason why it is extremely difficult to achieve a state of constant awareness. We have to do a lot of spiritual exercise just to free ourselves from the chains that have kept us bound for all these years without our knowing it.

☆ We have no idea of how long it will take us to realise our own reality or truth ☆

In fact, the purpose of all spiritual or inner work is simply to free you from all that binds you on the aspects of your being— the physical self, the emotional self and the mental self. I call these three aspects the holy trinity of the individual. It is only when you have harmonised and stilled these three aspects that you come to see your soul or spirit. Before this harmony of the trinity of the human being is reached, it is very difficult to become aware of what the soul or spirit within us is. In this moment, all of us exist at different levels of awareness already. We do not know what level we are at, do we?

We have lived different kinds of lives so far, and if you believe in past lives, then you realise that each one of us has lived many different kinds of past lives also.

You do not know what exactly you have brought with yoursel
in your balance of actions (karma) to date. You have no ide
about it. Thus, how can you ever know whether it is going t
take you one year or ten years of effort to reach your desire
goal? The true answer is that we just do not know. We hav
no idea of how long it will take us to realise our own realit
or truth.

Therefore, the questions that automatically follow are: How d
I perform my action when I do not know how long it will tak
me to become free? How do I live my life? How do I perforn
my spiritual practice?

The answer is that we must do our actions to the best of ou
ability, expecting that the final experience is going to come now
in this very moment.

We must act as if this is our last moment. Our effort must b
total, without thought of failure or disappointment.

Only when you have that kind of faith—that it is certainly goin
to happen—can you give yourself fully to the moment, to you
action.

If you expect, or if you believe, that you are going to perform
your effort totally but the final experience, enlightenment i
you will, is just not possible in this lifetime, then there is n
way that your action or effort will be full and total.

Action, no matter what it is, begins within you, based on the way you think, much before it becomes real or is seen in the external world. How you think is the

☆ We must act as if this is our last moment ☆

decider for how you act. This is the reason why all the spiritual Masters say that enlightenment is possible in this lifetime itself, so that you can give yourself totally, a hundred-and-ten percent, to what you are doing.

When you can do that, when you give yourself totally to what you are doing, when you have poured all that you are into what you are doing, a beautiful miracle happens. There is nothing of you left. And when there is nothing left of you, you become empty. And when emptiness happens, divinity follows. That is what I said in an earlier chapter when I advised you to stay empty. I reiterate that now. Emptiness is what you need and when you give yourself totally to something, you become empty. That is the secret of successful spiritual practice. To become empty so that God can fill you up.

Either you are, or God is!

There is a beautiful story from ancient India that brings forth this metaphysical truth very aptly:

A young seeker has spent many years learning from his Master. He is disciplined and dedicated in his study and practice, and his Master is pleased with him.

One day the Master calls that boy and says, "Perhaps you ar
now ready to meet God. Follow my direction to the house o
God and knock on the door when you reach there. Whethe
the door opens or not is not in my hands; that shall depen
upon you."

The seeker is excited and enthusiastically gets ready for hi
journey. He follows his Master's direction and eventually afte
many days of arduous travel he arrives at what he believes to b
the house of God.

He walks up to the door and knocks and from within asks
voice, "Who is there?"

"It is I," replies the boy and he gives his name, his Master'
name and even his parents' names and where he ha
come from.

But the door does not open.

Many years pass, and the Master asks the boy to try agai
saying, "Maybe now you are ready."

The boy again arrives at the door of the house of Go
and knocks, only to be asked the same question, "Wh
is there?"

His reply this time is, "It is I. But I have come to meet you."

Still the door does not open.

Many more years pass and this time the boy himself walks to the Master and says, "Master, I'm ready now. Give me your permission to go to the house of God."

With his Master's permission, he makes the journey and arrives at the door, only to be asked the same question once again, "Who is there?"

✫ Make yourself empty and then God will fill you up. To this I add, make yourself ready as well and God will surely arrive ✫

This time his answer is, "There is only you."

The door opens and the boy enters, to be merged with God.

There are three stages to enlightenment. In the first stage, you see only your identity, with perfect clarity, and are in search of God. In the second stage, you see both the identities—you and God. In the third and final stage, you see only God, in everything and everywhere, even in you.

Either you are, or God is. Make yourself empty and then God will fill you up. To this I add, make yourself ready as well and God will surely arrive.

Before you start on any journey, you have to know where you are going. The destination must be clear if you hope to arrive there. When you go to an airport, you do not just sit in an airplane that is before you. If you did that, who knows where you would land up? When you go to the airport, you already know where you are going and you then choose your flight accordingly.

Similarly, when you start the spiritual journey, be very clear in your mind what it is that you are seeking. Do you just want to feel better about yourself? That is a valid goal, too. Do you want to be more knowledgeable about the scriptures? That is a valid goal, too. Do you want to have better relationships? Do you want to be known as a scholar? Do you want to carry a label away with you that says 'certified so and so'? Or is your goal that you want to understand who you are? Is it that you want to know God? Is it that you want to have the experience that will end all other experiences?

What is it that you are after? Because what you are after is the destination that you are going to arrive at; that is what you will get. There is no point in emptying yourself and being all prepared for the 'experience' if you have no idea of where you are heading. Even as you begin your journey, and many times along the middle of it, it is essential to be very clear about the answer to the most important question: What are you seeking?

The Bible says, "Seek and you shall find." This one sentence declares a lot. It tells you clearly and unequivocally that if you do not seek, you probably won't find it. Thus, the seeking, the search for the truth, is very necessary, because it is the key ingredient that puts into motion a chain of energies and synchronistic events that eventually bring to you what you desire.

☆When you start the spiritual journey, be very clear in your mind what it is that you are seeking ☆

My Master would explain this in a very simple and nice way. He used to say that in traditional Indian homes, the mother is always cooking food in the kitchen, even though she has got young children playing out in the courtyard. Once in a while, one of these children starts crying. As the child starts to cry, the mother comes running to see what is wrong. But then she realises that nothing is wrong. The child is just crying for the mother's attention, or because he or she is feeling alone and discarded. So, the mother gives the child some toys, making the child happy again, and goes back to continue her work.

However, after some time, the child starts to cry again. Again, the mother comes out to see what is wrong and gives the child some other toys to keep his or her mind and attention occupied. She will probably give the child better toys this time. And if s/he is satisfied with those toys, she goes back to resume her work. It is only when the child does not want the toys any more and only wants the mother that she leaves her work, comes and picks him or her up, and sits with the child, giving

her full and undivided attention. Similarly, God will give yo
the worldly toys that you want to keep your attention an
mind occupied, for God is very magnanimous and ver
abundant. However, God will not come to you as long as yo
are merely satisfied with the small toys that have been sen
your way.

The whole concept that has been propagated and widel
believed for the past hundreds of years that spirituality an
abundance are divorced from each other is a misinterprete
one. Our ancient Masters, our great spiritual teachers, wer
all abundant people, very wealthy in both their thought an
their way of living. They said something and it simpl
happened. They thought about something and it became
reality soon enough. They declared a thing and soon it wa
reality. What is this if not abundance or greatness?

Spirituality is the root of abundance. The realm of spirit i
where abundance, prosperity and wealth of any kind begin. Th
universe is very benevolent, very gracious, abundant in all way
and lacking nothing but lack itself. So if it is only the toys c
this world that you want, if that is what you are truly seekin
and asking for, the universe is going to throw them at you soo
enough. And then it is up to you—are you happy with your toy
or do you want something more permanent? Or do you jus
want better toys? Maybe a Mercedes, not the Toyota you ar
presently driving. Or, do you want the One behind all the toys
the One who can truly make you complete?

When we start our spiritual quest, it is very important to keep the final goal in mind—what it is that we want? And be very clear that what you want is the actual experience of the truth, not just the knowledge of the truth. For, knowledge won't do it! Knowledge won't make it real for you. All the knowledge in the world will only give you a headache. This happens because when you read and you understand the different philosophies, and try to find the common ground between them all, you realise that people are talking different things. There are many Masters and many philosophies out there, all claiming to be the best and the only true way to God. So how do you put it all together in your mind as one complete and neat package?

This is another disease of the mind. It wants to put everything nicely together. Everything should fit very properly. And when you try to do that with spiritual knowledge, you find that it does not fit the way you expect it to. Spiritual truth will not fit into your mind the way your mind exists currently; your mind must expand to fit the truth.

God is large enough to accommodate all paradoxes and contradictions; the problem is that we are not. God is too big to fit into any one religion, but our mind and conditioning seeks only one way to follow, one path, one teacher, one truth.

> ☆ When we start our spiritual quest, it is very important to keep the final goal in mind—what it is that we want? ☆

At times, when you converse with spiritual Masters, they will say one thing and a few minutes later they are contradicting themselves, or so it seems. What does your mind do then? How can it accept it with its barometer of logic? It just does not fit. Knowledge and information is not what you are after. Always remember this—the truth shall free you, not knowledge. And the truth must be experienced by you, not just known or understood intellectually. Knowledge certainly is not what you are after as your final destination, experience is!

The Master is now ready to give some of his final lessons to his disciple. Over the years of training, the young boy had matured into a fine and intelligent adult, one who was capable of leading others to their own truth. But yet he had a few more chains of his mind to break. The Master summons him and says, "Often people will tell you that they cannot change their life, or their circumstances, because it is their destiny. It will almost seem to you that they have no concept of what free will is and indeed have no belief in it. You will feel that they see the externals of life alone and pay no heed to what's happening within them. It will look as if they have let go of their ability to be creators of their own lives and destinies. You will find them weak and impotent. In such times be patient and give them a teaching that frees their shackled minds."

"But what shall I give them that will make them believe and see again their power to create?" asks the boy.

"Teach them how to change their destiny. Give them this simple formula to change their so-called unchangeable destiny, if only given enough time and perseverance," says the Master. He then imparts the secret of the ancient Masters to the boy:

Change your thoughts to
Change your beliefs to
Change your expectations to
Change your attitude to
Change your perception to
Change your behaviour to
Change your actions to
Change your life to
Change your destiny

> ☆ God is large enough
> to accommodate
> all paradoxes and
> contradictions;
> the problem is that
> we are not ☆

"Teach them that what they call unchangeable destiny is nothing more than the collected force of all our actions, which originate in our inner beliefs and thoughts. Teach them that when they change their thoughts and beliefs, they have already started changing their destiny."

Changing your thoughts, perceptions, pre-conceived notions and your beliefs and attitudes will ultimately change your destiny. This is something you alone can do, with guidance from a spiritual teacher or guru. Begin to walk the path with no fixed ideas. Remember, we all begin this journey in the first place to arrive at something we cannot get anywhere

else—self-realisation, the experience of 'It'. So even as w
walk, it is imperative to keep our mind clear about the fact tha
knowledge is not what we are after, only realisation. And thi
will come when you are prepared to change from within.

Let me explain this point further, because clarity of th
destination will keep you firmly on the path and avoid th
frequent wandering of the mind into avenues that are wastefu
and unproductive.

Suppose I describe a mango as a round type of fruit, yellov
in colour, sometimes even orange-ish. I tell you that it has :
thin peel and has very juicy flesh inside, very sweet to th
tongue, very fulfilling on the stomach and, on top of it al
very nutritious. This is knowledge; information that I an
passing on to you. But, can I give you the taste of the mang
with all the knowledge that I have imparted? Can I make yo
taste the mango in actuality when I describe to you that it i
sweet and juicy? I may have tasted it many times before, bu
when I describe its taste to you, all I am doing is taking m
experience and putting it into appropriate words to make i
known and understandable to you; I am not making it you
experience. Not unless you have tasted it will you know it a
your truth. It does not become your reality till you have bitter
into it.

Conversely, even if you do not have all the knowledge abou
what a mango looks and tastes like and one day you come

across a fruit you have heard is a mango, you cut it and put a piece of it into your mouth, you will know the taste of it forever. You have had the experience of the mango now and surely you can now describe it to another. The important thing here is that only after the experience, which is your own, can you describe it as the truth, not before. Before you have had your own experience of the mango, at best you can describe somebody else's truth of the experience. Thus it is a description of another description, not of the truth, until you have tasted the mango yourself.

The other equally important thing to remember is that you do not have to eat the whole mango to know the taste of it. You can have just one bite of it and still know how the whole mango tastes. Imagine that you travel to the ocean, take an empty glass of water, fill it up and bring it back. And when you are back, say, a thousand miles from the ocean, you put it under a microscope and study it. You will find that all the properties of the ocean exist in that one glass of water.

> ☆ It is imperative to keep our mind clear about the fact that knowledge is not what we are after, only realization ☆

The water that you have brought with yourself is but a small part, a miniscule part, of that great ocean, yet it is just like the ocean. It carries all the properties of the ocean. If you taste it, it tastes like the ocean; if you study it, it has the nature

of the ocean. Everything is just like the ocean. But, it is not th
ocean. It is a glass of ocean water, that's all. Another importan
fact is that if you have tasted the mango once, you know its tast
forever. Even if you do not taste another mango for many years
you will always remember the taste of the one you have tasted
The experience is yours, once and forever.

This is how we arrive; with the experience of the experience
Just keep your vision focused on the ultimate experience. Jus
be after that one contact, that one taste of divinity. Becaus
when you have that, then everything else will fall in place, every
thing else will follow.

All the knowledge, one hundred percent of what you hav
learned before and retained in your mind for years, leaves yo
in an instant at the time of the experience of enlightenmen
You become empty, because of which, all of a sudden, all ne
things flow in. A new vision, the way God sees it, not the way yo
see it, flows into you. And you realize that before this you hav
simply been holding on, collecting and stuffing yourself wit
knowledge. Whereas the aim of spiritual practice is about be
coming empty, making some space within you. Do not let th
mundane things of this world get in the way of your emptiness
Constantly remind yourself that you do not want mere know
edge, not even knowledge about the experience. Be after th
realisation, be after the taste, be after the experience and per
severe till you have it. Nothing else matters; nothing else i
worthwhile.

One day in my own spiritual journey, I finally gathered up the courage and asked my Master about a question that had been troubling me for a long time.

☆ Just keep your vision focused on the ultimate experience ☆

I presumed that I had done many wrong things in my life, both consciously and unconsciously. I had hurt people, disappointed them, even profited at their expense. This is something we all feel at one point in time or another, don't we? It was bothering me, too.

So I said, "Master, I'm sure I have done so many wrong things in my life, both consciously and unconsciously, and now as I walk on the spiritual path, trying to do my best in every moment, I wonder, 'Is enlightenment going to happen for me? How will the force and the weight of all the negatives be overcome?' Please tell me."

He replied, "Think of a room, which has been in darkness for ten years—completely dark. There is no light coming in from anywhere. For ten years, it has been like this, year after year, day after day. But how long does it take to make it bright again? Just an instant! Come into this darkness of years and just light a match and there is the light. The darkness of ten years is gone in an instant. Do not worry; spiritual life is just like that. Keep doing your spiritual practice with diligence; you never know when enlightenment may come. Tomorrow may be the day."

There I had my answer! What a relief it was to know tha enlightenment is not bound by any rules of time, space an causation. What freedom it was to know that, in spite of all ou actions right up until this day, awakening and truth is sti possible for us. And it may happen in the next moment. As progressed further, I understood this process even deeper. Th reality is that to arrive at enlightenment you need two forces i your life, two complementary actions or energies in you spiritual journey for success. The first is your own self-effor and the second is grace.

Without these two coming together at one point in time, in on moment, enlightenment is not possible. If you do not put i your best and constant effort, grace does not come even thoug it is all around you. And if you do put in all your effort, bu you have no grace, the final experience still eludes you. Thus is a combination of the two energies that makes you one wit the truth.

Sri Aurobindo, the famous sage from India, put this in differen words. He said, "Two forces are always operating in this worl at all times and both influence the individual. One is th upward force, the seeking force, the striving for the truth, whicl is your own self-effort. You are always trying to rise upwards to go higher. And the other is the downward force, the force o divine grace, of the Master's blessing. And when you rise u enough because of your self-effort, one day, the grace come and pulls you up to the final and ultimate experience."

However, if you do not even try, or stay away from putting in your best self-effort and practice, grace and blessings will not descend upon you.

In fact, the more sincere and dedicated self-effort you put in, the more you attract grace to you. This is the reason why the three Ds are so important for they all apply to the effort that comes out of you.

Without sincere and dedicated endeavour from your side, the experience of enlightenment is not going to happen for you.

If you want to arrive at enlightenment, it is not going to happen just by itself. You must make the environment for it to occur. You must prepare the field, get the soil ready and then the seed will arrive to take root. You must try and do your spiritual practice to the best of your ability at every moment. Give your all to the action that you are doing. And, then, simply wait without expectations, for you never know when it happens. You just have to keep yourself open.

> ☆ Keep doing your spiritual practice with diligence; you never know when enlightenment may come ☆

The way to be totally open and to commit yourself fully to doing something is to believe totally that it is going to happen. If you believe it is not going to happen, you are never going to give a hundred-and-ten percent of yourself to it and then

you will never be empty. The secret is to be fully involved i
the action when you are doing the action and, the momen
the action is over, to totally surrender and open yourself t
receive, without expectations. When you can be this wa
enlightenment will find you. I conclude with one more stor
based on the conversation between the wise Master and hi
eager disciple.

"I now give you the new Ten Commandments for living a
extraordinary life," says the Master to his student.

The boy had come to him young and immature, almost like
sapling just taking root. But now he had matured into a fin
and strong tree, with roots deep into the ground; a tree capabl
of providing shelter and shade to many other traveler
passing by.

"Live your life by these principles and make yourself a
example for others to follow...thus you will not only tal
the talk, you will walk the walk," says the Master as he smiles t
himself.

And then he reveals to the boy the way to live an extra
ordinary life:

1. Never let the fear of loss stop you from the pursuit of gain
2. Never let the fear of pain stop you from the pursui
    of love.

3. Never let the fear of death stop you from the pursuit of living life to its fullest.

4. Never let the fear of separation stop you from the pursuit of union.

5. Never let the fear of failure stop you from the pursuit of success.

6. Never let the fear of negativity stop you from the pursuit of positivity.

7. Never let the fear of falling stop you from the pursuit of walking.

8. Never let the fear of crying stop you from the pursuit of laughing.

9. Never let the fear of tomorrow stop you from the pursuit of today.

10. Never let the fear of darkness stop you from the pursuit of light.

☆ The way to be totally open and to commit yourself fully to doing something is to believe totally that it is going to happen ☆

If you can be this way, enlightenment will surely find you.

Tip 7

Lose the drop, find the ocean

The seeker realises that only the taste
can reveal the heart of the mango

7 Valuable Tips for Those in Search of Awareness

Tip 1
Take it easy
A seeker is never in a rush

Tip 2
Stay empty
An enlightened person knows that
God exists in the space within

Tip 3
Trust in a higher power
A believer lives by the truth,
'God is for me, never against me'

Tip 4
Be persistent
Aspirants know that they alone are
responsible for their enlightenment

Tip 5
Put yourself on fire
A seeker will always strive intensely
to improve from within

Tip 6
Seek enlightenment everywhere
The enlightened person knows
that the world is a mirror

Tip 7
Lose the drop, find the ocean
The seeker realises that only the taste
can reveal the heart of the mango

Testimonials for Vikas Malkani and His Teachings

I thank Vikas for a fantastic teaching that was extremely inspiring for several reasons. First, the content; he summarised a vast amount of knowledge concisely and clearly. Then, his person al teaching style also added to the enjoyment. I absolutely loved his metaphors and stories, they are wonderful. At every turn they are inspiring, exciting and fun, always touching a chord at the heart level and leaving an imprint in the mind.

The bridge Vikas creates between the spiritual world and the physical life gives much weight to his teachings. People can relate the teachings to their lives. His calm yet imposing presence is also awesome.

Helene Liu, Hong Kong

Vikas' teachings were truly life changing. I signed up for his meditation course not knowing what to expect, but I found it to be beneficial on many levels.

First, I found a real sense of camaraderie and openness among the participants. Vikas brought us together in a very natural way and I feel bonded to the women in the group and look forward to seeing them all again.

Second, everything he said made sense to me in a very

practical way. His presentations are clear, he is an amazing storyteller and he has a great way of connecting with his students.

I also found the exercises to be very insightful. Using pencil and paper has always served me well when trying to sort things out in my life and his exercises provided a great framework for further study.

The teaching has helped me see my life through a different lens and I will be forever grateful to Vikas for that.

I have been a much happier person in my day-to-day life, in the manner in which I realte to my kids, my husband and everyone else, too. Thank you Vikas!

Jamie Hanna, USA

About the Author

Born and brought up in a business family in India, Vikas Malkani was the head of a large business enterprise when Awakening struck him at the age of 29. He has been called many things over the years: Spiritual Guru, Zen Master, Motivator, Mystic, Rich Monk, TV celebrity, Soul Coach and Reiki Master, to name a few. Other than that he is the founder o. SoulCentre and a best-selling author.

Today, Vikas is considered one of the world': leading contemporary spiritual teachers. He teaches people to be successful in all aspect: of life: the physical, emotional, mental and spiritual. His forte is to make the ancient wisdom of the spiritual Masters simple to understand and easy to apply to create a life o. health, harmony and abundance on all levels.

Vikas is a disciple of Swami Rama of the Himalayas and has been trained in the wisdom lineage of the Himalayan Masters that involve

www.vikasmalkani.com
www.soulcentre.org

the disciplines of meditation, spiritual wisdom and yoga. A gifted orator, he is a keynote speaker at many international conferences and summits. He leads life-transforming workshops for adults and is also the creator of the SoulKids™ programme for children, which has made thousands of confident and creative children worldwide.

Vikas Malkani has been interviewed in many international newspapers and magazines and been a guest on numerous television and radio shows. His writings on self-awareness and spiritual wisdom appear regularly in magazines on yoga, holistic health and the spa industry. His television show airs on prime time every night on a national spiritual channel in India.

About SoulWords™

SoulWords™ was created as an instrument to provide the wisdom needed for every individual's journey to wholeness and completion in all ways, be it in the physical, emotional, mental, spiritual or material aspects of ones existence. We are dedicated to publishing books and audio products that inspire and challenge us to improve the quality of our lives and our world. SoulWords™ publishes books on a variety of subjects including metaphysics, self-awareness, health, yoga, meditation, spiritual fiction, reiki, holistic healing, success and abundance, and relationship issues.

We encourage both established and new authors who provide quality material to work with us. We aim to bring their knowledge and experience in an easily accessible form to a general readership. Our products are available to bookstores everywhere. For our catalogue and other details, please contact us.

The Little Manual of Success

9 Essential Secrets of Self-made Millionaires

Best-selling author Vikas Malkani
shares with us in this new book,
The Little Manual of Success, the nine
secrets that will lead us to success.
These include taking responsibility
for your acts, believing in yourself,
rejecting mediocrity, following your
heart and being persistent. These
are the characteristics and qualities
of super-achievers. This manual tells
us that we, alone, will define what
success means to us. It also teaches
us to create a life of our choice.

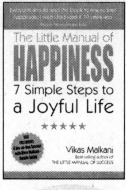

The Little Manual of Happiness

7 Simple Steps to a joyful Life

Best-selling author Vikas Malkani
shares with us in this new book, *The
Little Manual of Happiness*, seven
steps that can lead us to having a
joyful life, a life that is happy in the
true sense of the word. This manual
tells us to choose happiness; to live
in the present; to think happy
thoughts at all times and to make a
special endeavour to connect with
joy. A complete guide to happiness,
this book will change you forever.

The Little Manual of Meditation

15 Effective Ways to Discover Your Inner Self

Meditation is a very different, subtle and precise approach to locating your inner self, explains best-selling author Vikas Malkani in this book, *The Little Manual of Meditation*. He takes the reader through 15 steps that will bring positive results. Get ready to be freed from stress and enjoy a life of increased joy, clarity and awareness. Learn the simple techniques of meditation that will bring harmony to your life.

The Yoga of Love

11 Principles for Bringing Love into Your Relationship

Best-selling author Vikas Malkani
shares with us in this book, *The Yoga of Love*,
11 insightful principles to nurturing a long
lasting, meaningful and loving relationship
and experience. This book reveals
how the complexity of love and relationship
can be unravelled by applying these 11
principles, thereby gaining the love,
fulfilment and happiness that one seeks.
Read *The Yoga of Love* and life will never be
the same again.

Published by Marshall Cavendish, Singapore

The Yoga of Wealth

5 Spiritual Keys to Creating Unlimited Wealth

This book will transform your life in just one reading. Learn how to earn abundant wealth and achieve happiness through inner awareness, all of which can be complementary if you have the right attitude. The universe has an abundance of everything, you need to overcome mental blocks and realise your full potential to achieve a life of joy and abundance.

Vikas Malkani's books are available worldwide at www.amazon.com and in Singapore through Borders and Kinokuniya Books

Published by Marshall Cavendish, Singapore

Dear Reader,

Avail of an unbelievable opportunity to have a private one-to-one session for an hour with the author of this book. To benefit from this opportunity, please answer the following questions and send them in by post or email to Vikas Malkani at:

SoulWords Publishing Pte Ltd
Newton Post Office P.O. Box 183, Singapore 912207
soulcentresingapore@yahoo.com.sg

A draw will be held to choose the winner of this opportunity

1) Name _____

2) Mailing Address _____

_____

3) Email _____

4) Telephone Numbers _____

5) Where did you purchase this book from?

_____

6) What is the most important lesson you learnt from this book?

_____

7) What subjects do you read?

_____

8) Would you like to be informed of Vikas Malkani's other books and upcoming workshops? _____